Confessions Of A Perplexing Teacher

Jacklyn Wright

India | USA | UK

Copyright © Jacklyn Wright
All Rights Reserved.

This book has been self-published with all reasonable efforts taken to make the material error-free by the author. No part of this book shall be used, reproduced in any manner whatsoever without written permission from the author, except in the case of brief quotations embodied in critical articles and reviews.

The Author of this book is solely responsible and liable for its content including but not limited to the views, representations, descriptions, statements, information, opinions, and references ["Content"]. The Content of this book shall not constitute or be construed or deemed to reflect the opinion or expression of the Publisher or Editor. Neither the Publisher nor Editor endorse or approve the Content of this book or guarantee the reliability, accuracy, or completeness of the Content published herein and do not make any representations or warranties of any kind, express or implied, including but not limited to the implied warranties of merchantability, fitness for a particular purpose.

The Publisher and Editor shall not be liable whatsoever...

Made with ❤ on the BookLeaf Publishing Platform
www.bookleafpub.in
www.bookleafpub.com

Dedication

This book is dedicated to Granny Donna and Papa Harvey Allen. Granny only had a middle school education and always encouraged us to make sure we finished school. Papa always had a smart remark and helped me to understand just how important every single word can be.

Preface

The idea for this collection of poetry came to me one day while I was monitoring a 4th grade class during a state test. Everything was so quiet that any small amount of noise seemed excruciatingly loud. I began jotting down a few of these sounds that I heard throughout the test and, before I knew it, I had written "Quiet, Testing in Progress." I had a few ideas and beginnings of poems about different school topics in my writing journal; so, I began brainstorming book title ideas for a collection of poetry that centered around the things I see and hear and learn every day as a teacher. This gave me direction each time I sat down to write. Some of the drafts I had of other topics soon became tailored to fit into this collection as I edited and revised them. I hope you can relate to and enjoy each poem included in your own way.

Acknowledgements

First of all, I would like to thank God for providing me with an open mind and placing me into a country that allows me to freely write whatever ideas that may come.

Second, I would like to acknowledge my husband, Aaron Green. Without his love and support, I could hardly find the motivation or the time to complete this collection.

Also, I would like to thank my family, friends, and coworkers for being so encouraging after my first collection of poetry was published. That book revealed many emotions that I never enjoyed talking about and everyone was extremely supportive.

Finally, I would like to thank my students for unknowingly serving as the subjects of much of this collection and for constantly asking when I planned on publishing a second book of poems and relentlessly pushing me to finish this collection.

1. Quiet, Testing in Progress

"Shhh!"
"No talking during the test."
Someone sneezes.
Someone yawns.
A chair squeaks.
Feet rustle under a desk.
A toilet flushes in the bathroom next door.
There's another yawn.
Someone sighs.
Someone coughs.
The bell rings.
Lockers slam in the hallway.
The bell rings again.
There's another cough.
Someone sniffles.
Another child yawns.
Knuckles crack.
There's another sniffle.
Pages turn.
Another chair squeaks.
More feet rustle under desks.
A pencil falls to the floor.
The quiet shouldn't be so loud.

2. Counting to Ten

Juan's tooth
reformed five
secs aft
Sven ate
nine tins.

3. Plans of a Teacher

Daily
Weekly
Monthly

Lesson
Substitute
Individualized

Medical
Dental
Vision

Weekend
Summer
Future

New
Changing
Canceled

Retirement
Family
Heavenly

4. A Millennial Teacher

I am an American Millennial teacher.
I feel misrepresented, being from rural Oklahoma.
I believe this country was built on the backs of the working class.
I worry that our leaders have strayed from God's guidance.
I dream of the simpler times of my childhood.
I strive to instill values in the youth of today.
I am an American Millennial teacher.

5. The Outdoor Classroom

The sun is blinding,
But my skin feels warm.
My hair blows in the breeze,
But it's nice to breathe fresh air.
The trees have been winterized,
But the clovers begin to flower.
Recent floods erode the ground,
But beautiful patterns are left behind.
Leaves scatter the ground,
But dandelions are poking through.
Distractions are everywhere,
But so is inspiration.

6. A Lesson in Love

There's something different in his eyes
when he looks at you.
A hunger yearning for your touch...
the same hunger is in you, too.
You tell yourself that he's the one
you've been waiting for
As he walks across the room
after locking the door.

There's a new sensation traveling
through your body with each kiss.
As he tenderly lifts your shirt,
he asks if you're sure about this.
The uncertainty inside you comes
to the surface and begins to grow;
But the passion has you enchanted
and won't let you say no.

He lays you down; your heart pounds
and your body feels tense.
He asks if you're alright --
the initial pain causes you to wince.
No more words until he's finished
and, it's true, you'll never forget it.
Your first time is like no other,
but that doesn't mean you'll never regret it.

7. Students of Spring

The beginning of Spring
can be so exciting,
with the trees and flowers budding
and the children outside playing.

The days are no longer slow,
as the warm breezes blow,
green leaves begin to show,
and relationships are able to grow.

The wind is the encouragement
that carries each moment
of nature's empowerment
and each student's development.

8. An Eternal Lesson

Lord, I'm cold.
Oh, how I long for beautiful Mays
filled with lovely, fluttering jays.

Lord, I'm so cold.
Oh, how I long for summery days
filled with brilliant, shining rays.

Lord, I'm still cold.
Oh, how I long to escape this maze
filled with a suffering, sorrowful haze.

Lord, I'm too cold.
Oh, how I long to meet your gaze
filled with a radiant, luminous glaze.

Lord, I'm no longer cold.
Oh, how I love my eternal days
filled with your joyous, everlasting praise!

9. If You Know, You Know

What is something you don't know that you don't know?
I know this has to be a trick question.
How can I know?
I can't know.
Who really knows?
My husband probably knows.
Could I ever really know?
I want to know.
Do you know what I don't know that I don't know?
Somebody knows.
Does it even matter if I know?
Nobody would know.
Do I really want to know?
I don't know.
Do I even need to know?
If I don't know, nothing can change.
Can I learn what I don't know that I don't know?
It doesn't matter if I know.
Do I really know anything?
I know that I am curious about everything.
What if I do know, but I think I don't?
I would never know.
How can I teach what I don't know?
There will always be something that I don't know.

10. Indoor Recess

I hear the rush of rain and the rolling of thunder.
I peer out the window as droplets leave trails on the glass.
I feel the gloom created by the grey, overcasting clouds.
I suppress a yawn brought by soothing sounds on the bricks.
I see water flowing and puddles forming on the playground.
I sigh and stretch because the showers show no signs of stopping.
I wish we didn't have such wet weather just as much as the students do.

11. A Child's Wish

A bicycle
A stuffed bear
Some new toys
A friend to play with

A chess set
A PlayStation
Some fun games
A home to play in

A baby doll
A kitchen set
Some pretend play things
A family to love me

12. Sit and Think

I sit around and think
About pens and pencils
About ink and erasers
About transcribing drafts
By writing words that wink.

I sit alone and think
About lines and verses
About songs and lyrics
About composing beauty
By writing words that wink

I sit outside and think
About sounds and muses
About rhyme and rhythm
About describing sights
By writing words that wink

I sit with you and think
About your eyes and sparks
About your voice and smile
About adoring you
By writing words that wink

13. Graduation

What expectations do you have for yourself?
Do you wish you had experienced more?
Did you accomplish your goals for this part of life?
Do you have firm beliefs and strong faith?
What do you anticipate in the next chapter of your life?
Do you feel afraid or discouraged about moving forward?

Look forward to everything the future holds.
Do not regret the things you didn't do.
Make ambitious goals for every part of life.
Stand on your beliefs and let your faith guide you.
Aspire to do great things in the next chapter of your life.
Don't hold back! The world will gain so much from your courage.

14. Acceptance

The world will never accept you.
You must accept that.
The world rejects everyone.
You must live with that.

The world will not help you succeed.
You must accept that.
The world tries to hold everyone back.
You must overcome that.

The world gives you as little as possible.
You don't have to accept that.
The world will allow you to create joy.
You must embrace that.

15. Schools

Some
Children
Have
Other
Obligations in
Life

Students learn to
Create
Hope for the future
Of
Our
Lives

Studying
Can
Help the
Ordinary become
Outstanding
Lifelong learners

16. Books

textbooks
library books
children's books

required reading
leveled reading
easy reading

nonfiction books
fiction books
picture books

hardbacked
internet-backed
paperbacked

boring books
interesting books
illustrating books

reading to teach
reading to learn
reading to inspire

17. Parents and Children

Parents teach their children how to explore the world and become an individual.
Parents teach their children the language of the world and how to use their voices.
Parents teach their children how to handle the world and control themselves.
Parents teach their children the views of the world and how to present themselves.
Parents teach their children how to treat those in the world and to accept accountability.
Parents teach their children the ways of the world and how to succeed in it.
Children teach their parents how to succeed in the changing ways of the world.
Children teach their parents about the lack of accountability for the way they treat the world.
Children teach their parents how to present themselves based on the views of the world.
Children teach their parents the difficulty of controlling themselves while getting a handle on the world.
Children teach their parents how to understand their voices in the language of the world.
Children teach their parents how to become individuals while exploring the world.

18. Teaching

Talking in front of staring eyes
Expecting the same effort from students and parents
Asking questions without a response
Creating lesson plans just to change them
Hoping to reach at least one child each day
Investing time and money into other people's children
Never giving up on the future of our youth
Getting little to no appreciation in return

19. The Lifecycle of a Backpack

Fabric and materials are bound together in the factory.
Employees place the backpack into a box to be shipped.
The box is loaded onto a truck to be transported across the country.
The truck is unloaded at the retail store the backpack is placed on a shelf.
A child catches a glimpse of the backpack.
A parent purchases the backpack for the child.
Books, notebooks, paper, pencils, and laptops fill the backpack.
The backpack is carried, thrown on top of lockers, and dropped on the floor.
The side pockets, straps, and zippers begin to wear thin and rip.
A bus driver finds the backpack under a seat with loose paper and empty folders.
The backpack is tossed into the dumpster with other trash from the bus.
The dumpster is emptied by a garbage truck the next day and taken to a landfill.
The backpack is no longer visible amidst the many mountains of materials.

20. Lunch Time

Children lining the long rows
Air smelling of chicken and potatoes
Food remnants scattering the floors
Echoes bouncing off the walls
Teachers enforcing the school rules
Empty spaces separating students
Rectangular trays clattering on tables
Incessant voices chattering in groups
Agreements transpiring over lunch trades

21. Time for Summer Break

Summer break begins mid-way through May,
But it might as well begin on April's last day.
After Spring break in March, the kids are wired,
But the teachers are over it and tired.
Testing is finished and there are so many field trips,
But lunches become sandwiches and chips.
The weather gets warmer and days get longer,
But the will to get out of bed doesn't get any stronger.
Time is taken by graduations, banquets, and benefits,
But staff work hard while the students push their limits.
It's all fun and games the last week of school,
But it just drags on while we dream of the pool.

www.ingramcontent.com/pod-product-compliance
Lightning Source LLC
Chambersburg PA
CBHW070050070426
42449CB00012BA/3210